GW01401294

First published in Great Britain by Hodgson Press 2010

Hodgson Press
PO Box 903[A]
Kingston upon Thames
Surrey
KT1 9LY
United Kingdom
enquiries@hodgsonpress.co.uk
www.hodgsonpress.co.uk

A CIP catalogue record for this book is available from the British Library.

ISBN: 978-1-906164-13-3

Illustrations by Patrick McManus.
Sketch of Patrick courtesy of Judy Prince.

READY MIXED AGGREGATE

Hodgson Press

POEMS BY PATRICK MCMANUS

DEDICATION

JANET SALLY SAM EVA ROSIE JAN CLARE
KIERAN MICHELLE MIKE LOTTIE DOMINIQUE
ALASTAIR MO ROY MIRANDA TANSY DES
PATRICK TILLY DARCY ROBIN CHRISTINE
AND THE REST OF THE FAMILIES ANN VW
RUSSEL T BERNI DAVE WHATLEY WRITERS
MERTON POETS

CONTENTS

FISH FOR DINNER

when
he mentioned
perhaps fish for dinner
she enthused yes!
a *bouillabaisse!*
or
calamari – deep fried squid!
coquille st Jacques
– scallops in pretty shells!
coulibiac – russian pie!
goujons – crumbed in strips!
gravadlax – scandinavian pickled salmon!
matelote – french fish stew in wine!
sole bonne femme – in mushrooms!
or even a *sole meuniere!*
lightly fried in butter sprinkled
with lemon juice and herbs!
but
he said surprise!
been to chippie!
and proudly opened
his warm folded
vinegar scented
newspaper

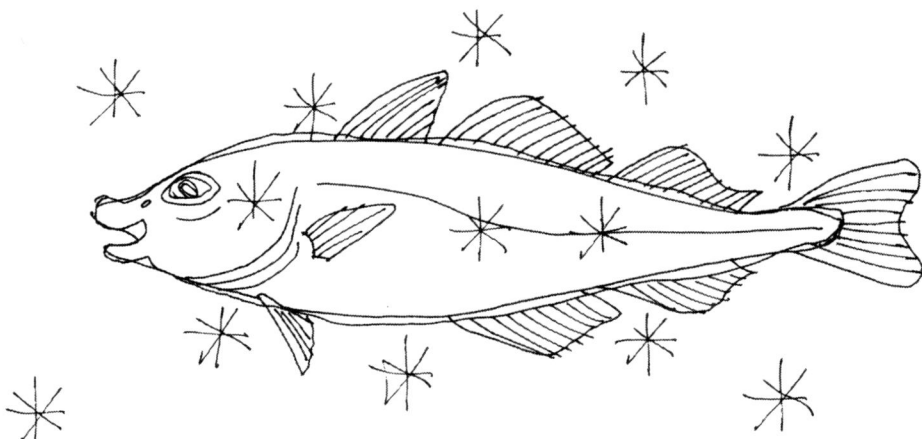

IT'S ALL RIGHT

It's all right all right for you
you've got houses homes
central central heating
beds cosy all cosy
hot water bottles and things

but I am a tree
I don't complain

stuck out in all weathers
snows and storms all windy
rain rain wets me rotten
sun all hot burns and blisters
frost freezing sap zapping

but I am a tree
I don't complain

birds birds twittering wittering
awful noises awful nestings
bugs eat me moulds growing
dogs don't talk to me about dogs

but I am a tree
I don't complain

my roots my roots are playing me up
my trunk carved carved up
my branches fumbling failing
my twigs splitting splitting ends
my leaves are falling falling out

but I am a tree
I don't complain

so on a cold wintry night
with your fluffy slippers on
with sitcoms chatshows cheery
it's all right all right for you

but I am a tree
I don't complain
_____

IN THE CAFE

in the café
transport café
on each
and every table
spotless formica fields
the Condiments
are set out lovingly
precisely exactly
in military formation
standing to attention

Vinegar Bottle -cast glass
Red Sauce-Brown Sauce
the plastic squeezy twins
so fat and jolly
Sugar Container
-nobbly glass with shiny
chrome top dispenser
and smaller in front
the halflings
First Pepper then
his Brother Salt
-glass white capped
pot bellied and
last at the far end
Square Ashtray
-stainless steel
practical all set
corners dimpled

together this team
so smart they form
and stand so proud
a little squad willing
cheery ready to serve
waiting welcoming.

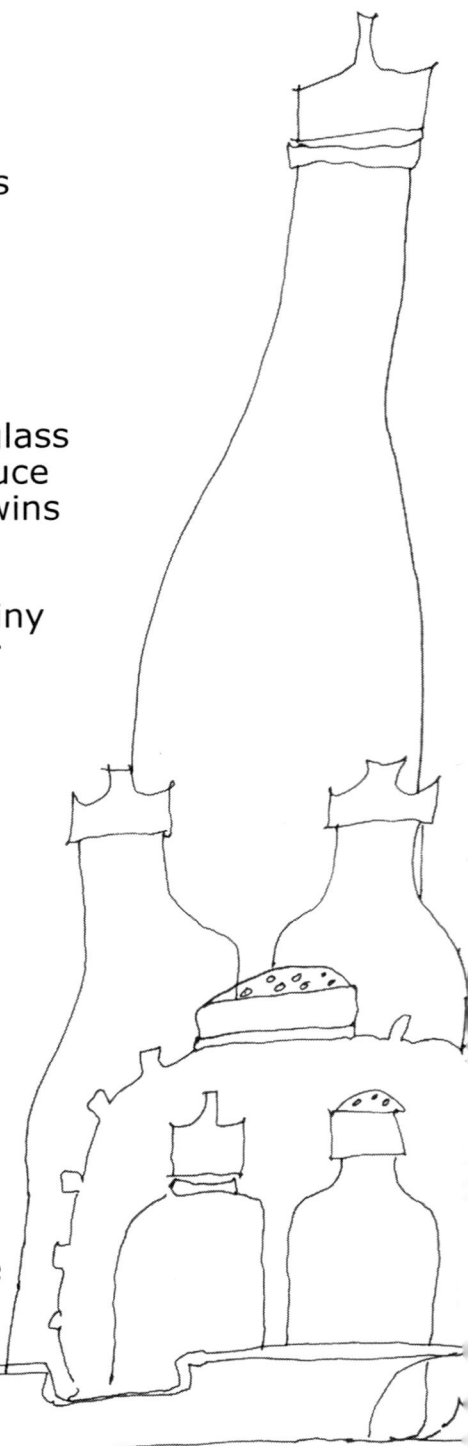

_____

MATHS

when he
asked her
his baby
she sitting
with her teddy
and school
Barbie lunchbox
'how was the maths
homework going?'

her reply of

` ≈ ≡ ≤≥
∞ √ ∫ Σ
‖ · ! /
∴ < =∞
° ± u ^
≈ ‖ · ∞ ≡
+ = < ? >
☺ Daddy!'

was not really
appreciated
by daddy himself

but
mummy said
'darling where's
π pet?'

_____

CAT

he said
it's that cat!
neighbours' cat!
bloody cat again!
he shouts
he shoos
he claps
he stamps
outraged

said cat
saunters up
purrs purrs
rubs his leg
plays with
his shoelace
rolls on back
sticks feet in air
and wiggles
appreciated
contented
deleriously
happy.

_____

RIVER

his great
river of life
with its waterfalls
gorges torrents
had been dammmed
at others been piped
channelled canalled
eddied backstreamed
even estuaried
but
at the moment
it was a
shallow stilled
oxbow lake
and
evaporating fast
with no hope
of rainfall

———————

LOOK-LOOK AT ME!

look-look at me!
I'm the New Central Heating!
high energy efficient!
state of the art performance
I'm digitally computerized
modern ultra modern!
touch of a button!
clean so clean!
I'm wonderful!
eat your heart out

and
look at me
I'm the Fire
in the Old Fireplace
Hearth and Home
with my friends the Flue Grate
and battered Mantelpiece
the christmas and birthday card
home nick knack centre
holiday souvenir displayer
mini bottle collector
family focus

you central heating lot
just come and go
suffer breakdowns
you're unstable
needing constant help
from lackadaisical
cowboy robber engineers
I've seen four of you
fur up rust up bleed
pipes leaking disgrace
radiators spewing

you can't even
survive a power cut
then get outdated
get discarded
carted off to die

you talk of performance?
when could you ever
comfort -make toast?
warm sad hearts
nurture dreams
inspire love and passion
engender revolutions
with cheery dancing flames
an open fire's friendly glow
casting shadows
burn tear stained love letters
all you give off
is carbon monoxide
and horrid noise

I've got history
that counts you know
in these edgy times
we go back to the caves
had decent paintings
then on the walls
when mammoths
sabre toothed tigers roamed
I protected them then
they know that

oh yes so blithely
at this moment
you prattle away
sing your little tinny tune
but all your gas
is on the blink
is running out
don't eco friendly me
I'll still be here
built in integral
to the house
part of the family
when you are
nothing but a
rusting tin can
buried in a vile methane
corrosive acidic stinking
rotten polluting
befouled landfill site

then we will hear
less of that
look at me!

10

HOSE PIPE BAN

re the
hose pipe ban
seeing his worry
his concern
she hastened
to reassure him
that it was
still permitted
for him to
use his
male member
to pass water.

———————

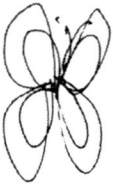

BUTTERFLIES

he had
butterflies
in his stomach
and every
now and then
would hiccup
and one
would appear
out of his mouth
spread it wings
flutter around
the small room
soon it was full
a whirl a swarm
of flying beauties
unfortunately
all this
did not help
with his
job interview

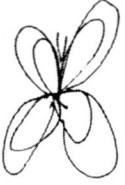

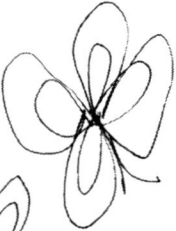

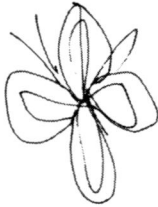

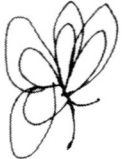

———————

FLY!

rousing
he said
said to her
there's a fly!
fly in the room!
and she
half awake
drowsily
all crossly
muttered fly?
what do you mean
mean a fly?
are you
referring to
an Agaric,Alder or Bee
A Dung,Fairy or Horse
a House,Ichneumon
a Lace Wing,Robber or
a Scorpion, Snake
a Warble or Stone
or just my
my fly orchid?
and turned over
drifting back
back to sleep
fast asleep
snoring
before he
could
reply.

_____

BOTTOM OF GARDEN

he always
laughed at her
when she talked about
fairies at the bottom
of their garden
and then he stupidly
made the mistake
of investigating
on a moonless night
at midsummer
and
now found himself
totally surrounded by
belligerent sprites pixies
malevolent goblins gnomes
a venomous old hobgoblin
two skinhead troll leprechauns
punk ill natured pucks and kelpies
and worse
about to be impaled
trampled by an outraged
foul frothing mouthed
mean one eyed scabious unicorn

———————

YOU RING

you ring
out of the blue
and say that
you want to
commit suicide
and have I
any ideas
how to
best do it?
that you
had been
up in the attic
but it was
no help there
and that
you have
forgotten
how to cook

——————————

WROTE

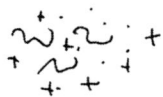

they wrote
their poems
like silversmiths
or as goldsmiths
with precious materials
fine and intricate work
set with precious stones
so delicately adorned
embellished

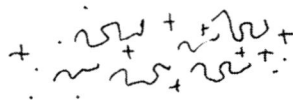

He wrote
his poems more like
a village blacksmith
at home with solid anvil
sledgehammer and swage
a good old forge hearth
with true iron blast pipes
a quenching trough bosh
stripped to the waist
working up a good
healthy sweat

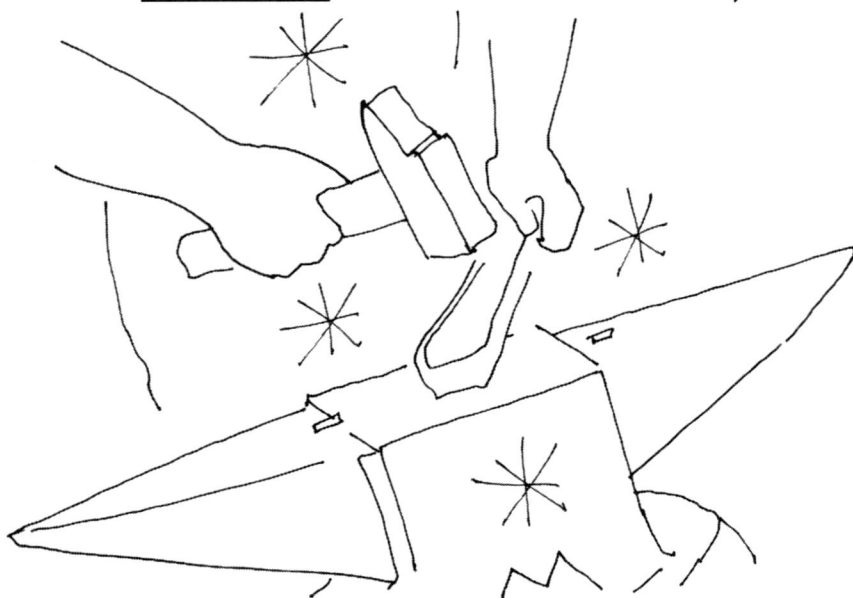

——————————

KNIGHT

he was
her knight
in shining armour
and he rode out
each morning
from their castle
to do battle
with dragons
and other monsters
he travelled
across forests
fields and into
the village
and at the station
he boarded
the crowded
commuter train
inspectors and others
tended to develop
a blind spot
in his case
and ignore him
his faithful steed
double handed sword
serfs and vassals
and pack of hounds
but even so
slain dragons
however fresh
were not
encouraged
on homebound
rush hour
evening trains

TRIED

painfully
desperately
he tried
to find
a straw
in a large
needlestack

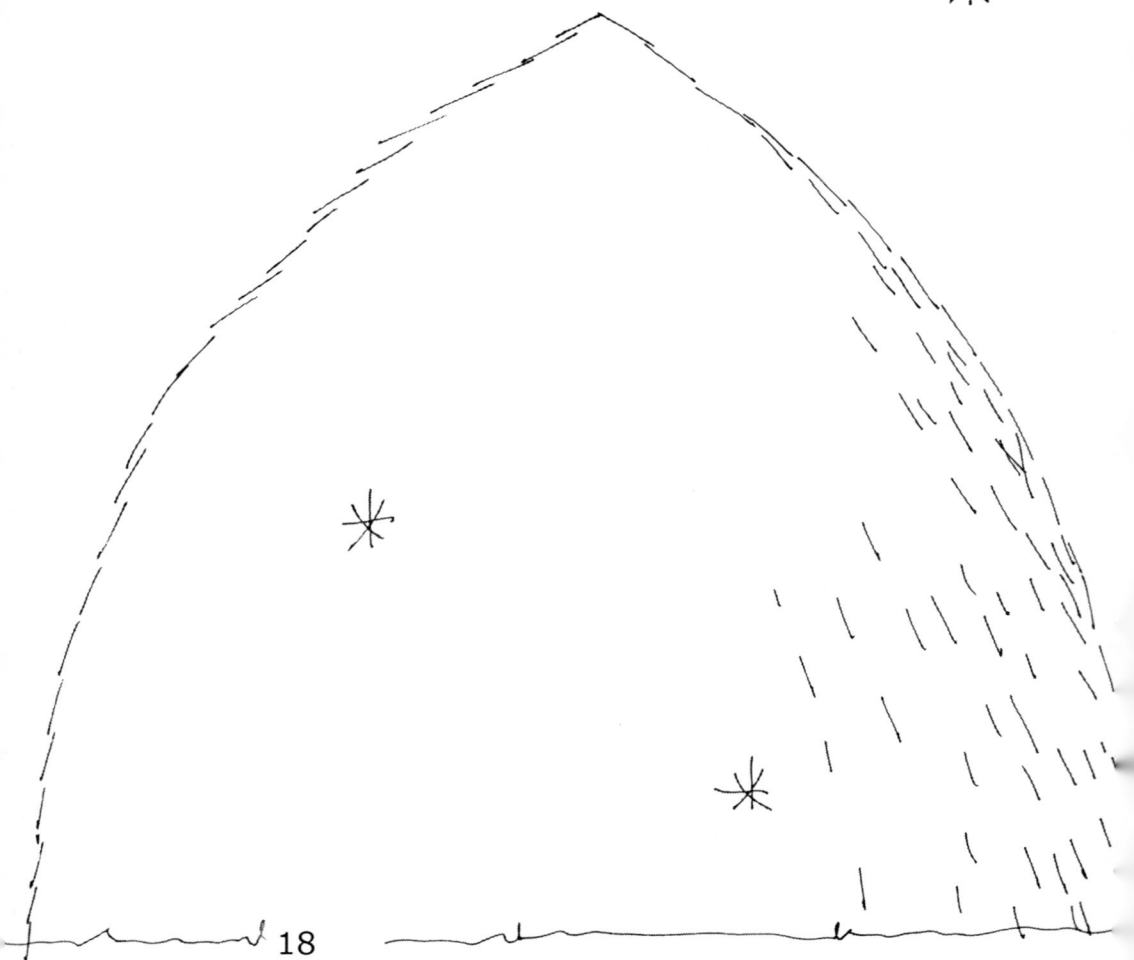

———————

FAIRYTALE

it said
turn
turn again
Dick Whittington
and after
some thought
and
charmed words
he did
but
by mishap
into a frog
but
fortunately
was later
kissed
by a passing
well endowed
princess

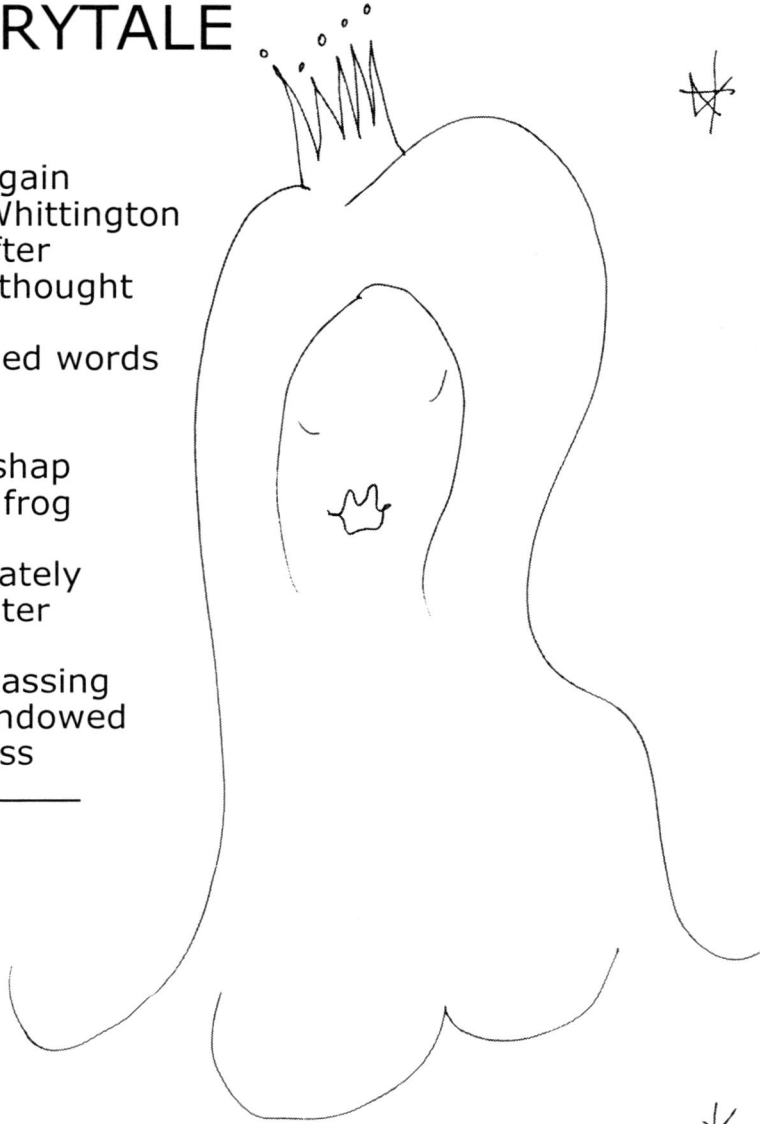

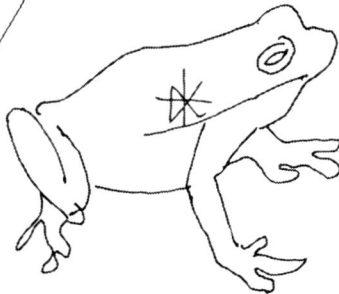

———————

WORDS

early
that morning
when he
came to write
he was dismayed
that he had
used up
most of
his dictionary
and
only had a
few words left
like
umquhile
villicitation
wakerife
ywroke
and
zinziberaceous
and he really
could not see
how he could
use these
successfully
in a romantic
love poem

AFTER

after
His Holiday
with Her
and Driving
and Cottage
and Dorset
and Rain
and Rain
he lay in
the recovery
position
chilling out
in the dark
for some
days
listening to
calming music
drinking lots of
very weak tea
and slowly very
gently stroking
his cat

———————

TROUSERS?

when she asked
who do you think
wears the trousers
in this family?
he modestly
patted down
his miniskirt
to just above
his sweetly
dimpled knees
and cutely
smiled

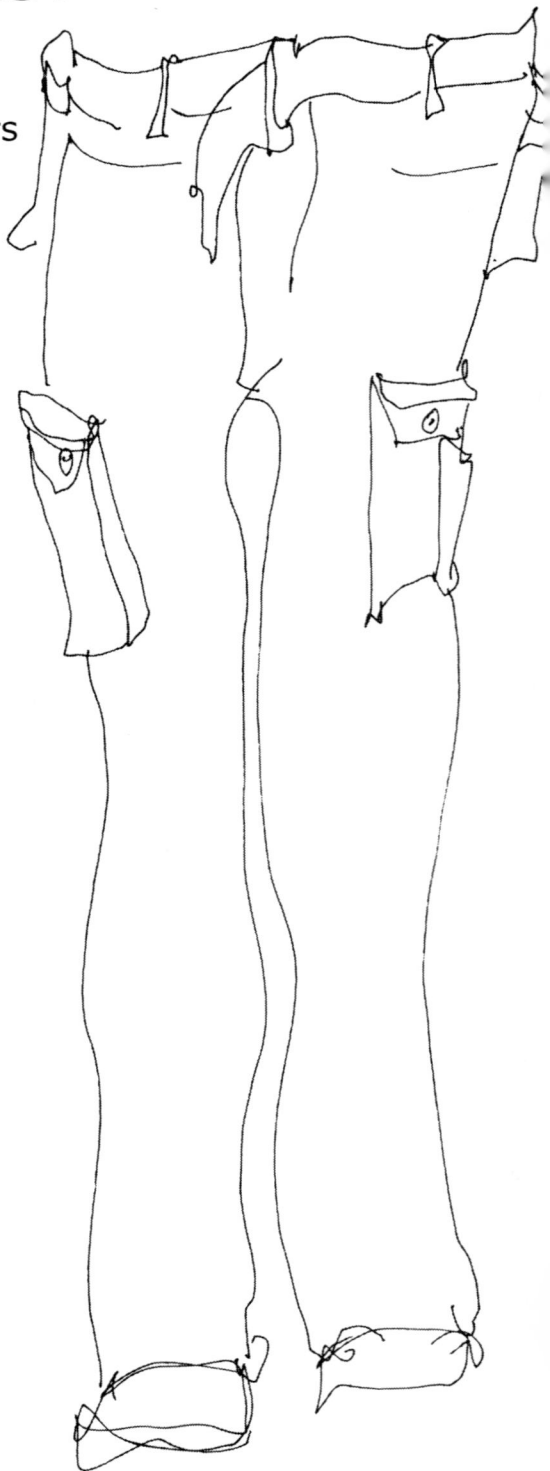

———————

MUSIC

he rushed
back in
from his outing
and delightedly
mentioned that
he had heard
a really lovely
piece of music!

and she said
well what was it?
a calm idyll?
magnificent counterpointed fugue?
religious oratorio?
soaring strident organ?
toccata −cantata-canon
partita suite-extravaganza?
nor a rondo nor even a
wildly ecstatic rhapsody?
short bagatelle −barcarole ?
harmonical passacaglia −fantasia?
divertimento- bold concerto grosso?
short sweet intermezzo?
neat etude −lively scherzo?
requiem mass tone poem?
nor even a nocturne -pastorale?
elaborate arabesque?
or even other forms
and she beamed at him
questioningly

he was
not sure but it
sounded a bit like
'twinkle twinkle
little star'

RECESSION!

recession
it was a
recession
they would
no longer
be able to
go abroad
own a car
go to restaurants
and much else
and he happily
breathed a sigh
of relief

———————

24

UPLIFTING

She said
just for once
couldn't you write
write me a poem about
something uplifting?

and
he inspired
wrote lovingly
in free verse
enthusiastically
ecstatically
about her
new bra
featuring
bold plunge!
pink bordello!
underwired balcony!
completely bounce free!
shapely figure support!
seamless soft cup!
T back action cut!
UV multiway!
pure cotton micro fibre!
ultra feminine power print!
minimum breast coverage!
her exciting new
designer styled bra!

and then
he eagerly
so proudly
presented his
poem to her!

———

CRYSTAL

he said to her
that on his way home
he had seen such
a beautiful crystal
she said
what sort of crystal?
triclinic?
monoclinic?
orthorhombic
tetragonal?
cubic holohedral?
cubic hemihedral?
tetragonal ?
pyramid hexagonal?
stretched trigonal?
he replied that
it was sort of
sweetie shaped
and a
lovely blue
like her eyes
_____

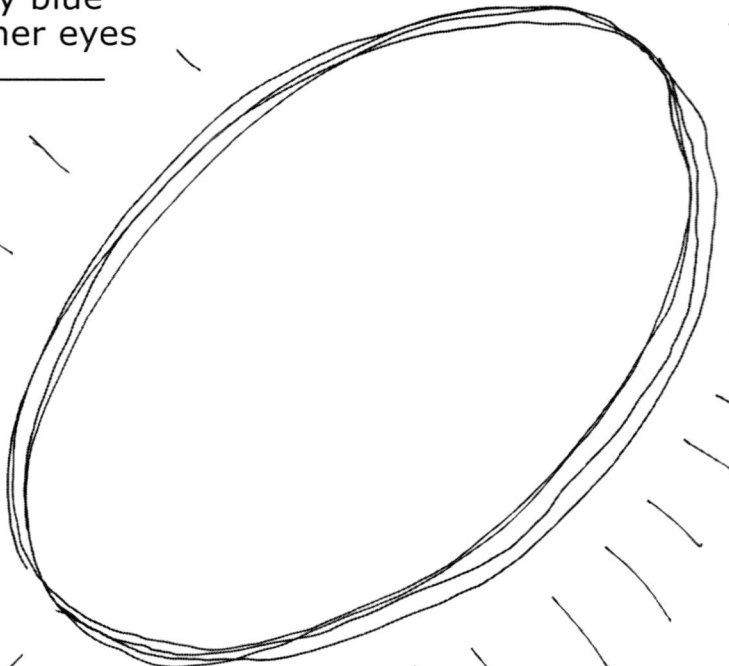

RELATIONSHIP

in their
relationship
he felt
like a proton
in the
Hadron Collider

and that
they were
sadly experiencing
to greater
or lesser degrees

Q elusive Higgs bosons,
CP-violations
String Theories
Electromagnetism,
Electroweak Symmetries
Gravity Symmetries
Dark Matter
and Dark Energies
Supersymmetric Partners
Hierarchy Problems.
Grand Unification Theories
Weak Nuclear Forces
Strong Nuclear Forces
Fundamental Forces
Elementary Particles
Supersymmetric Partners
Higgs mechanism elementary particles
and so much worse Masses
and Decays of the Quarks

and he was
feeling rather
pessimistic

_____

WITHOUT

without
her constant
helping hands
total backing
support unquestioning
total commitment
undying loving
throughout
the years
he would
not now
be in such
a total
mess

———————

POSTING

when he got
to the post office
to post his fresh
newly written
poetry anthology
there was a sign saying
prohibited items to post
such as explosives
corrosives pesticides
infectious substances
toxic substances
oxidising materials
radioactive materials
environmental waste
indecent obscene or
offensive material
and particularly filth
and he hastily
decided to deliver
each copy
laboriously
by hand

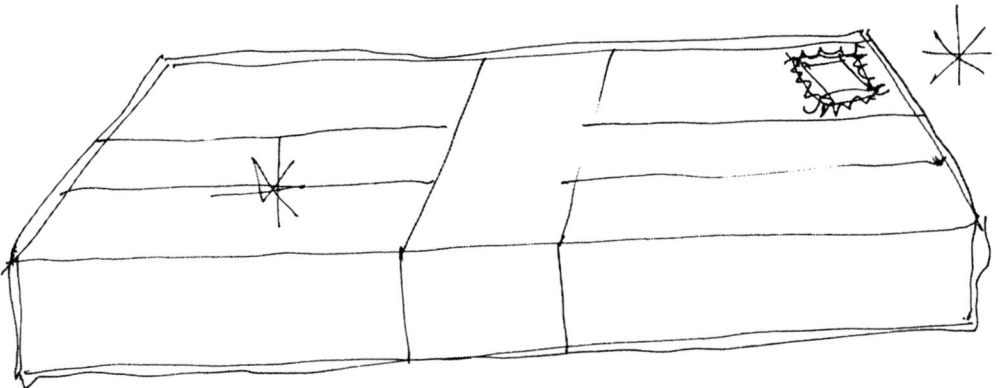

WRITING

when she said
that the writing
was on the wall
for him to see
he went
and looked
and could not
but notice the
appalling spelling

_____

SUPPORT

when he
elderly gentleman
turning and suddenly
coming inadvertently
face to face
with her large
magnificent cleavage
he became
all dizzy
thinking of
flying buttresses
swirling galaxies
then overcome
near fainting
had to
immediately
grab for support
and it was
fortunate that
she was wearing
a superfirm
doubly reinforced
extra duty
sports bra

he later
woke up in
intensive care
his pacemaker
wildly beating
on red alert

———————

HAMMER

He asked her for a hammer
She smart efficient smiled
and said well we've got a
Brick,Claw or Club ?
and some lovely
Copper,Engineer's or Kangos?
neat new polished
Lath,Magnetic or Panel Beating?
a good selection of
Pins,Quarry or Rawhide?
and just arrived
Scaling,Scutch or Slaters?
and for a big boy like you
Sledgehammers up to fourteen pounds
double faced heads only or ash shafted?
but then perhaps it was a
Spalling,Tornado or our Warrington?
ball cross or straight pein?

or
he said
perhaps a mallet?

well dear
she beamed delighted
Rawhide nought to six?
Bossy, one and a quarter to four?
Carpenters, beechwood four to six?
or last of all a beauty our
Tinmans, box head, cane handled
one and a half to three inches?
but you would need a
moleskin cloth
that's extra?

and so
wrapped presented
armed for mothers day
to a craftswoman superior
and with a moleskin cloth
that's extra
he made his way home

but he
wisely left
the choice
of a saw
to later
to another time
delayed
deferred.

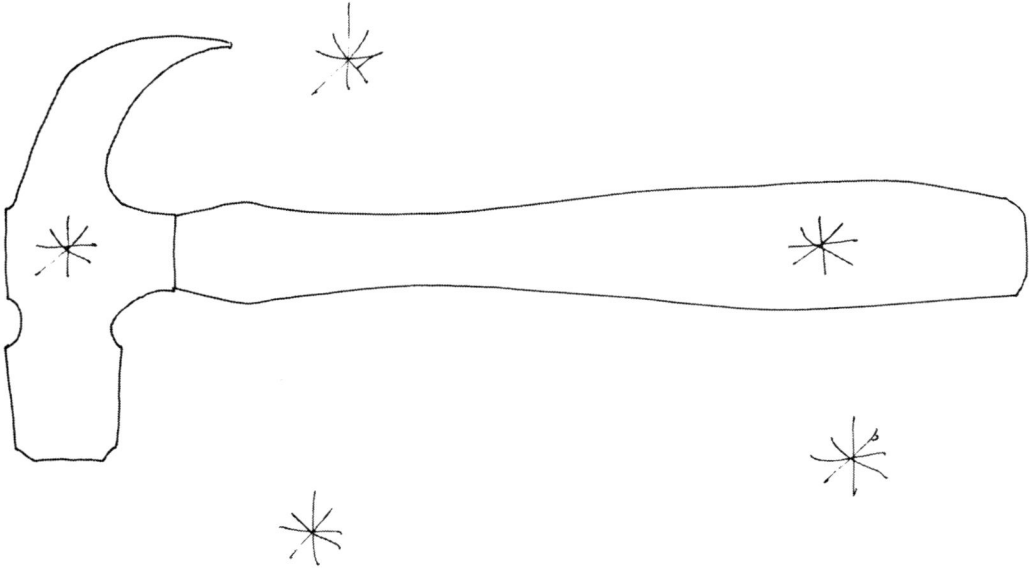

_____

MEDICINE

'the only medicine
that you need
is to get married'
said his mother
somewhat as usual
sanctimoniously

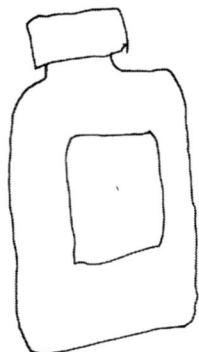

he later much later
tentatively examined
the detailed
information leaflet
that came with
his mail order bride
'take not more
than three times daily'
and
'definitely not to
exceed the stated dose'
his troubled eye
also rested upon
'possible side effects'
'feeling dizzy faint or sick'
and
'especially do
not use after
the expiry date'

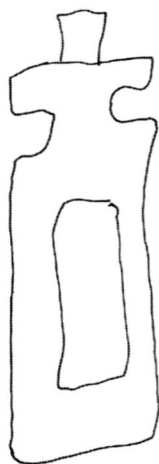

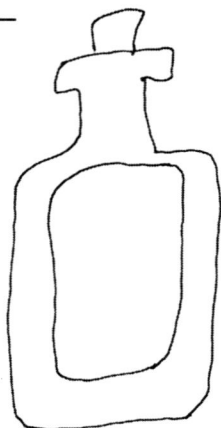

———————

SWORDS

one day
feeling vexed
prickly,testy
he was sorely
tempted to cross
swords with her
but
when she proudly
showed him
her sword collection
including
blades, steels, cutlasses
broadswords, claymores
foils and sabres
let alone daggers
dirks, stilettos, poniards
lances, javelins. halberds
pikes, tridents and harpoons
and
also cups, trophies,
awards of merit, citations
prizes for proficiency
for use of same
he thoughtfully
reconsidered

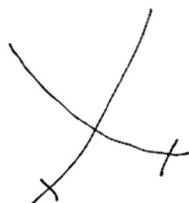

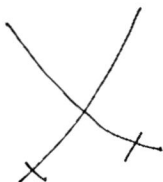

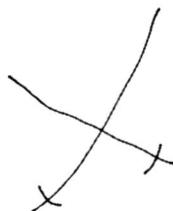

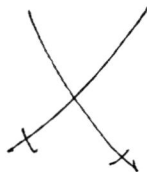

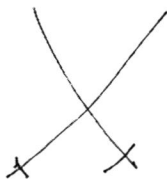

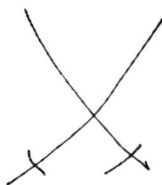

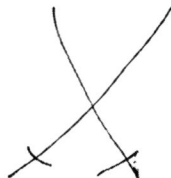

LACED

fondly
his busy
flustered mother
said but with
some hesitancy
you are five
you must learn
to tie up
you own shoes
to go to school
and left him
on his own
all on his own
to do just that
well first he tried
a good old Reef Knot
then an Overhand
a Figure Of Eight
a Square with a Single Sheet Bend
then a Double Sheetbend and Garrick
was tempted by a Bowline
a Triple Bowline he could not resist
then moved on
to the Hitches
starting with
a Half-hitch not very secure
a Timberhitch for heavy work
then
his favourite Clove
Round Turn and Half Hitch
but getting now excited
approaching Lashings
first the Square
the Diagonal
and finishing with a Shear

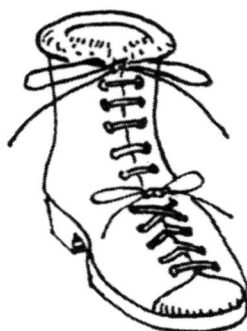

and then his mother
flustering back
to untied laces
what not done?
you hopeless boy!
gave him a kiss
and did one Granny
and a very poorly
executed lopsided
Basic Shoe Lace
and sent him off
these he corrected
and was a bit
bit late

late for school
but his teacher
forgave him when
when he did
his popular
demonstration
of Fancy Knots
to the class
of a Compound Chinese
Lantern Cord Knotting
embracing especially
the Three Part Crown,
Four Part Crown Butterflies,
Two Cord Diamond, a Two Wall
and others, finished with
a Three Ply Turk's Head!
to wild applause

later
after school
on the way home
he lovingly
restored
his Granny Knot
and lopsided
Shoe Lace
greeted his busy
flustered mother
and asked what's
what's for tea?

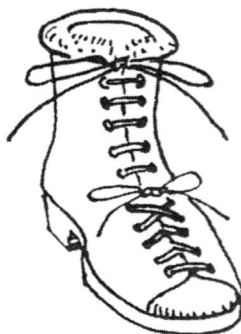

DRIP DRIP

drip drip
drip drip
tap drips
drip drip
drips tap
can't sleep
drip drip
sleep drip
can't dream
drip drip
dreams drip
drip drip
drip night
night drips
drip drip
drip drip
drip demons
demons drip
drip drip
drip trip
trip drip
drip drip
flip drips
drips flip
drip drip
drips flip
flip drips
drip drip
dawn drips
drips dawn
drip drip
day drips
drips day
day day
drip drip
drip drip
drip.............

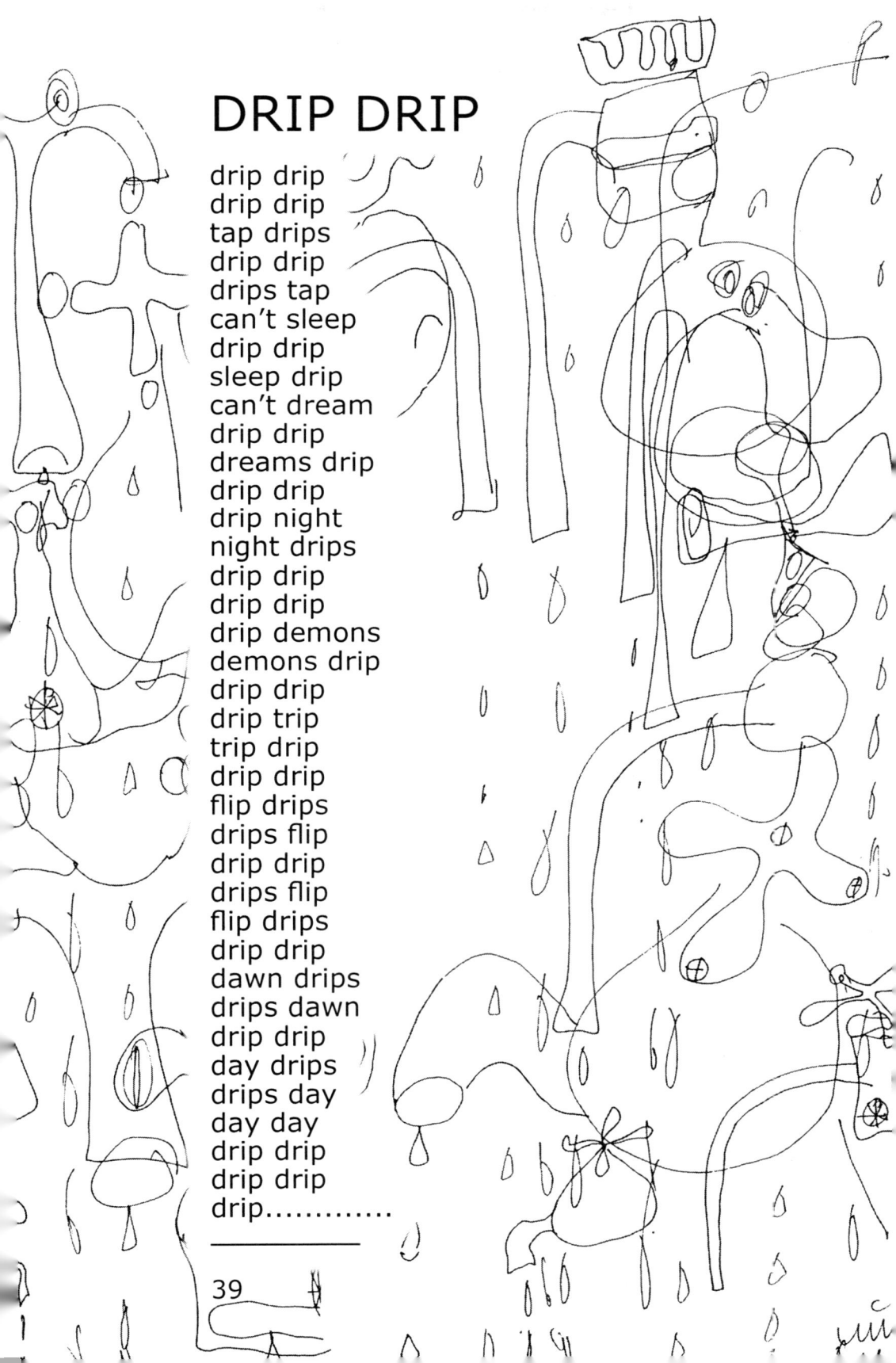

39

CONSIDERATION

she considered
with some satisfaction
that her ex husband
would be particularly
vulnerable to
swine flu

———————

THE MOON

the moon
pulled the sea
the earth
pulled the moon
the sun
pulled the earth
the galaxy
pulled the sun
the universe
pulled the galaxy
and he
pulled the birds
but only
partially
successfully

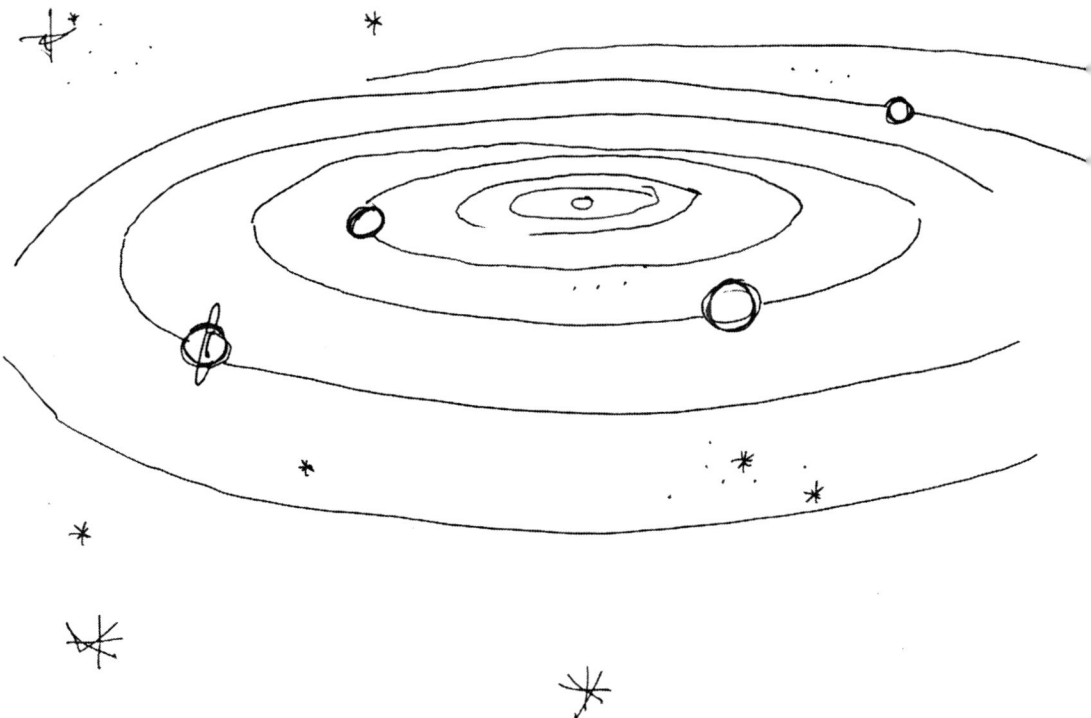

WAITING

when he
finally
got home
she was
waiting for him
with an axe
in her hand
but he disarmed her
with a cheery smile
and a bunch of
sweet scented flowers
which she accepted
putting them into
a delicate china vase
then carefully snapped
the heads off each bloom
then putting them
into her blender
before serving
dinner

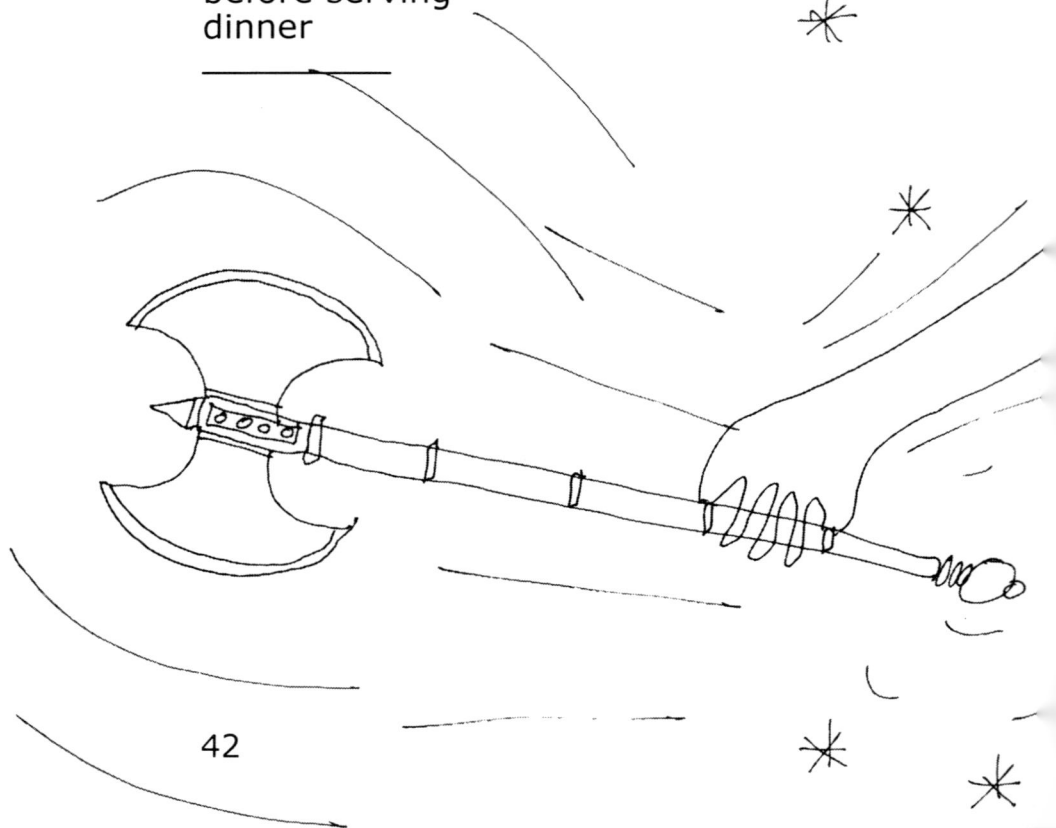

BREATH

he found that
his bad breath
did wonders
in ridding
the broad beans
of black fly

EIGHTY-THREE

eighty-three
eighty-four
eighty- five
he rushed in
and asked her
what was
what was he
going to do
with the rest
of his Life?
but she said
with a sigh
eighty- six
can't you see
eighty -seven
that I am
counting stitches
eighty- eight
and can't be
eighty- nine
bothered with
with trifles
ninety
ninety- one
ninety-two......
....
———————

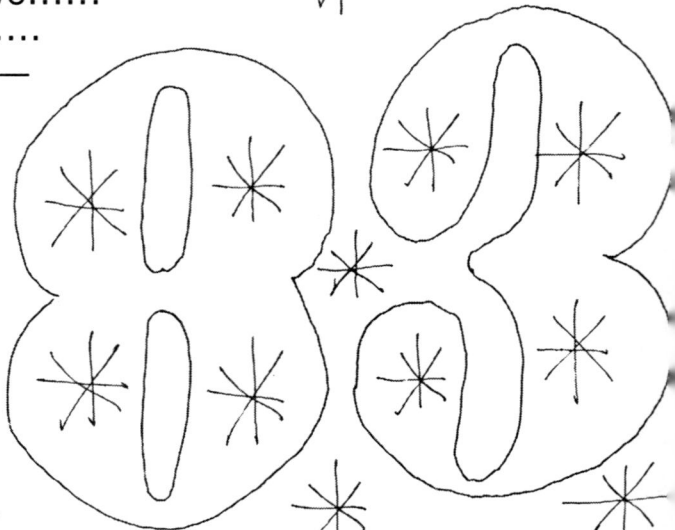

SIDING

each
day
 he
  kept
     on
    trying
         to
       get
        to
          the
            other
             side
            of
             the
               page
                but
                 as
                   soon
                      as
                       he
                        was
                       getting
                      anywhere
                        near
                        he
                       got
                  knocked
                 battered
              bashed
            pounded
         whacked
        buffeted
       depressed
  downhearted
beaten
back
home
again
again
_____

LOVE POEM

totally
enamoured
he had
a love poem
tastefully
beautifully
tattooed on his
male member
but then
unfortunately
discovered
that she
could not
read English
and
that he
had sadly
run out of space
for a translation

SOMETIMES

sometimes
he was up
sometimes
he was down
but at the moment
he was hovering nicely
like a hummingbird
poised over a flower
sampling sweet nectar

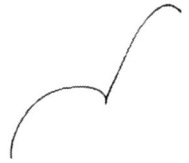

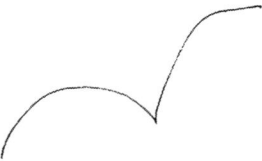

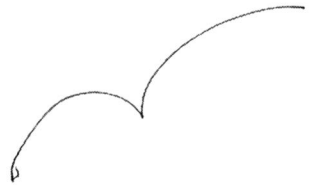

WEDDING

when the couple
in the marriage
registry office
gave their names
as
Mills and Boon
the Registrar
then paused
but only
ever so
slightly

———————

EEK!

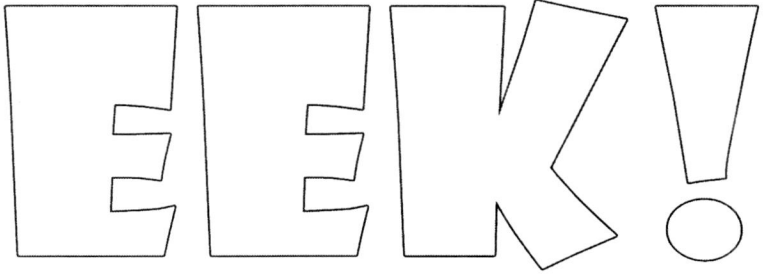

she cried

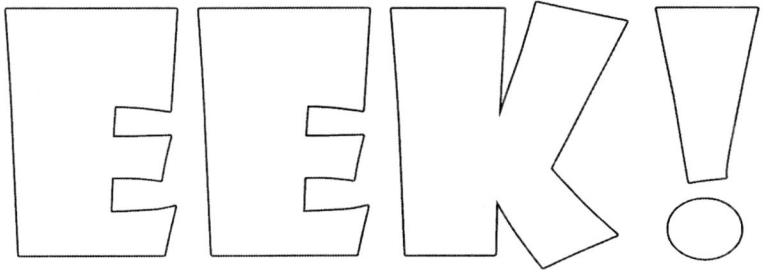

she cried again

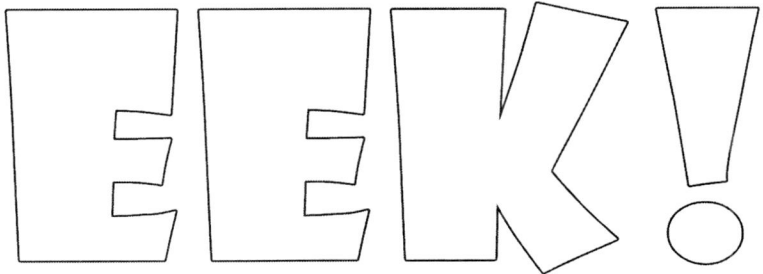

but by then the terrified mouse had fled

49

LIBRARY

in his house
he had a
large collection
of books
seldom read
even referred to
late one night
he came in
with a slim
attractive paperback
there as a ripple
of envy outrage
among the huge
neglected tomes
pages stirred
covers creaked
movements made

later
was found
a man's cruelly
battered body
beaten by blunt
heavy objects

in his library
every book neatly
in it's own place
bar one new
sadly torn
ripped crumpled
slim paperback

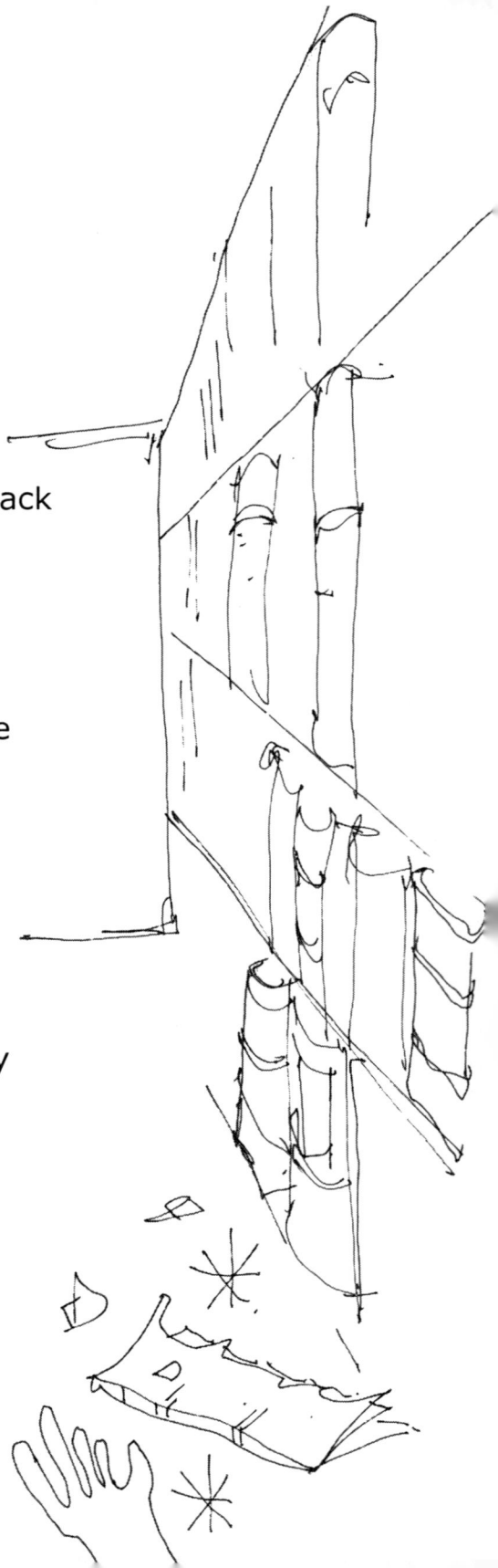

———————

HE USED

he used
to like
to go out
to travel
go abroad
cinemas-theatres
exhibitions
and all that
sort of thing
but these days
just give him
a pad of paper
and his good old
favourite pen
and peace
and quiet

———————

DRIVING FAST

he was
driving fast
through life
his life
and then
suddenly
coming to a
cul de sac
a dead end
screeching to
an emergency stop
leaping out of the car
finding a footpath
then deciding
immediately
to join
the ramblers
association

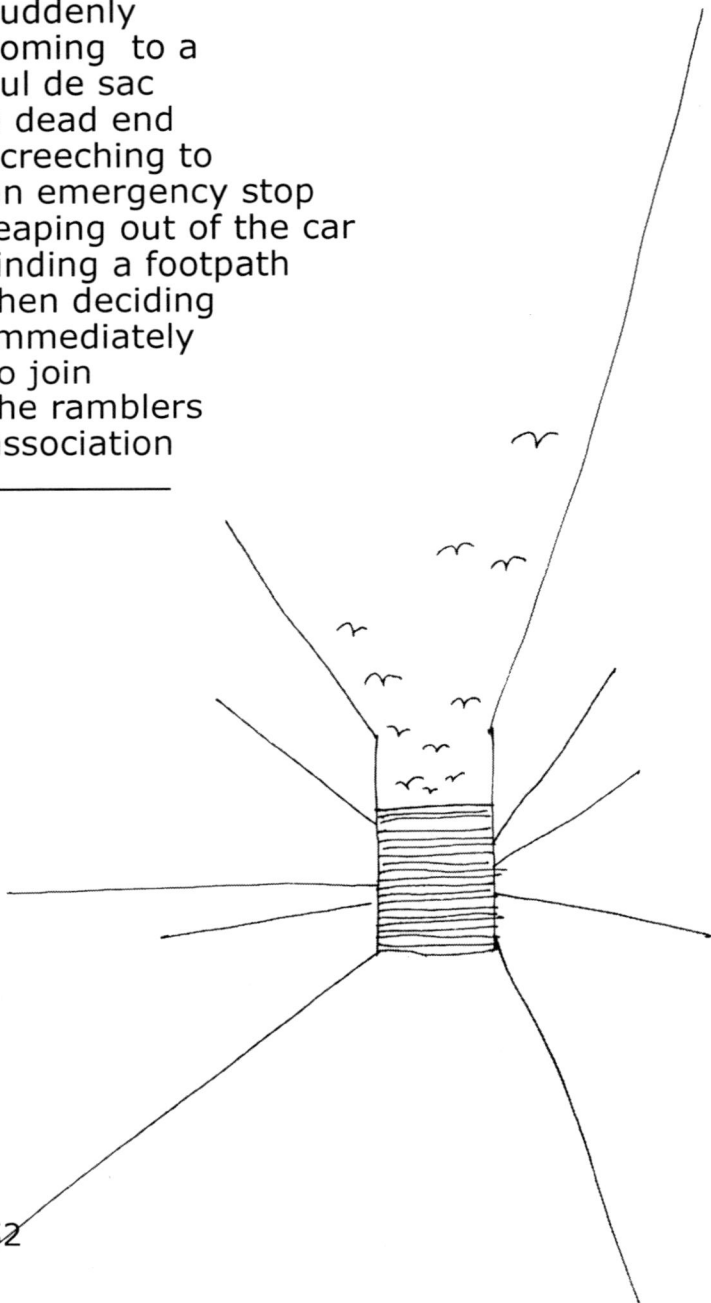

EARLY

her early careers
as a mud wrestler
pole dancer
and lion tamer
proved to be
of great use
and comfort
in her marriage

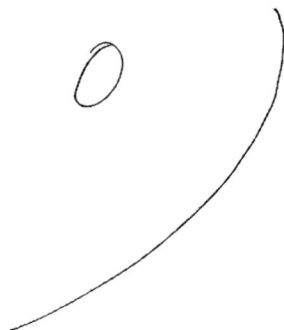

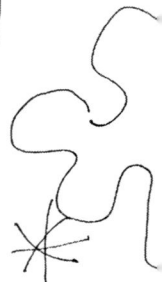

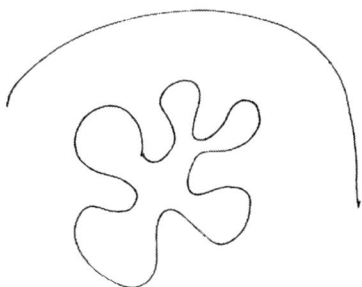

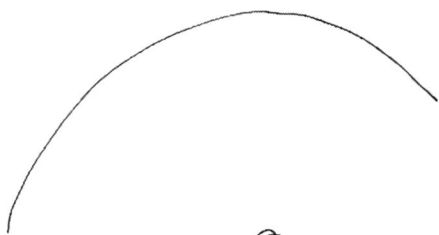

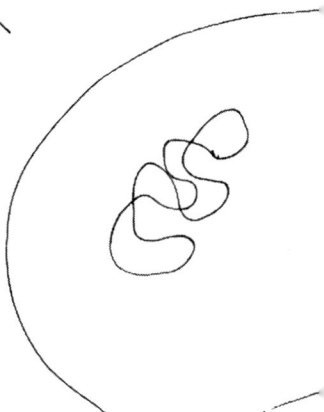

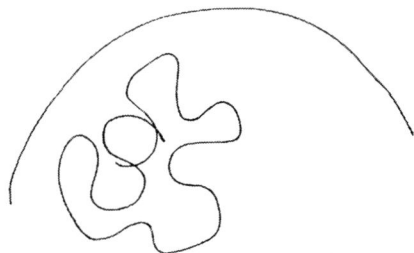

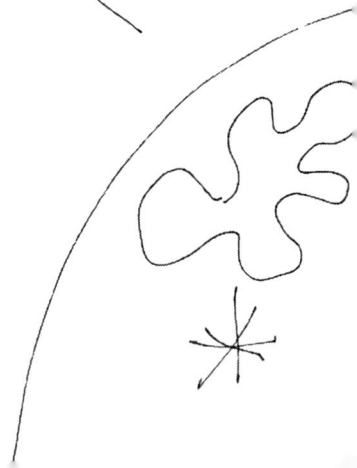

CORDON BLEU

she was a
cordon bleu chef
and she decided to
bring all her skills
to their lovemaking
first she carefully
marinated him
then
brule with caramelised sugar
fard well stuffed
farci further stuffed
fines herbes
infused –steeped
liason thickening agents
macerated soaked
jardinière garnished with vegetables
and of course *soused pickled*
puree mashed and pulped
then quickly delighted him being
beat -chopped -creamed
diced -pared -poached
simmered and sated
fantastic experience!
leaving him gasping
but her overuse
of her cast aluminium
precision balanced
heavyweight tenderizer
proved to be
his undoing

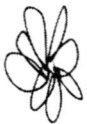

———————

ANNIVERSARY!

this year
the couple
decided to celebrate
their wedding 's
silver anniversary
by getting some
really high class
plastic surgery
but due to a
slight mix up
in the paperwork
those people
in admin!
he came out
with beautiful
enhanced breasts
and she with an
enhanced penis

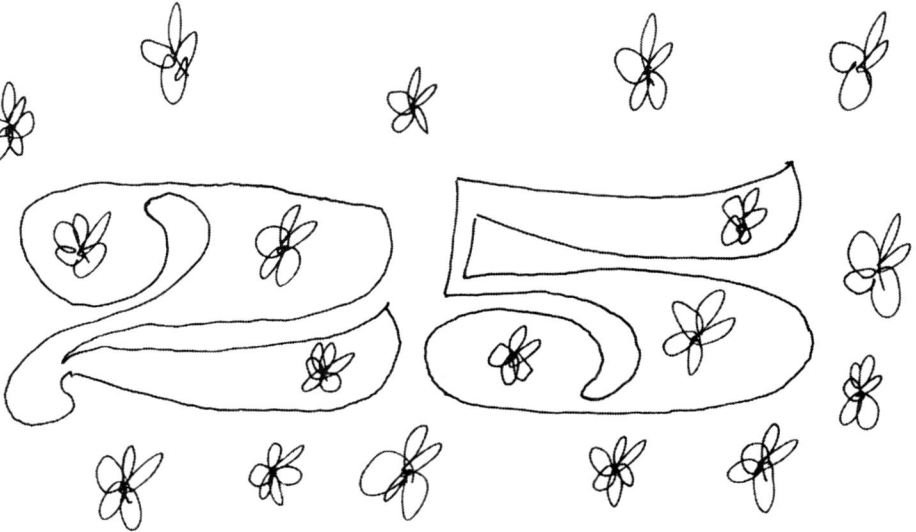

———————

METASEQUOIA GLYPTOSTROBOIDIES!

when she got
back all enthused
from her refreshing walk
in the local park
to her new boyfriend
of only one night standing
him left watching his footy
on the deadly telly
she waxed lyrical
about the
slender *betula pendula!*
magnificent *quercas robur!*
brilliant *acer pseudoplatanus!*
quaking *populus tremula!*
weird *ginkgo biloba!*
then finally about the
prehistoric awesome
metasequoia glyptostroboides!
and only discovered in 1941!

she then
observed
the blank look
of incomprehension
upon his face

and
she then
muttered
they're trees!
bloody trees!
trees!

———————

CHRYSANTHEMEMUM

he rushed
back from
the flowershow
enthused that
he had seen
a lovely pretty
chrysanthemum
and
she said −really?
was it a single?
or an incurved?
or intermediate?
not a reflexed?
nor even fully reflexed?
or anenome centred?
or classy pompon?
or spoon shaped ?
quill shaped?
but surely not
a rare spider form?

he beamed at her
it was yellow!
and fluffy
just like your
lovely pretty hair!

UFO

when
the UFO
landed
in his back garden
on his flowerbed
the neighbours
sympathised
that he was annoyed
and even outraged
but to have attempted
to wheelclamp it
was considered
somewhat
foolhardy

GOOD NEWS

good news
granddaughter
at five years
frilly and pink
has dropped
her ballet class
entrechat
jete -pirouette
and now wants
lean and mean
to move on
to martial arts
hajime!
yama zuki!

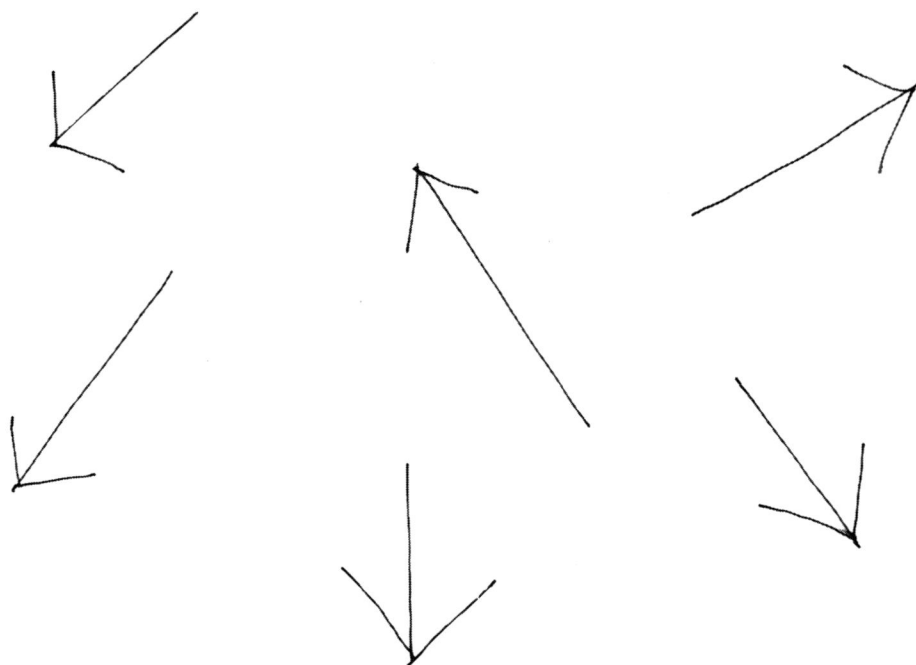

LOSER

she knew
that when she
took up with him
that he was
a bit of a loser
but even so
the final score
still shocked her

———————

BY CHANCE

He
by chance
in the middle
of the night
peered out
through his lacy
curtained windows
and saw
under the full moon
of the clear sky
on his fine
ghostly lawn
surrounded by it's
herbaceous borders
topiaried hedges
the Worms so
elegantly dancing
a pavane or galliard
swaying so gently
perhaps he could hear
faintest of courtly
strummed music

He
decided not
to tell Her
about it in
the morning
but
fondly regarded
the casts
left behind
little ringed
reminders

―――――

ALL INSPIRED

all inspired
he unleashed
the full gamut
of the mighty dams
of his creativity
but was rather
underwhelmed
by the small
tentative drip
that emerged
very slowly
and so soon
dried up

_____

ONCE UPON

once upon a time
not so long ago
there was a
poor royal prince
trapped up a
steep rocky mountain
in a creepy damp cave
captured by a dragon
and the little girl
who lived in the valley
far down below
heard about it
and put on her
mountaineering geer
and bravely set off
after her breakfast
up the cliffs
using martial arts
sorted out the dragon
and saved the poor prince
then she taught him
how to climb down
do knots that sort of thing
and then they were
great friends ever after
later she married a
handsome lifeguard
and became a world
famous speriologist
and lived happily
ever after

———————

HE HAD BREAD

he had bread
he had butter
he had cheese
he had tomato
and he had pickle
but he also
only had
his family's
sixteenth century
six foot compound hilted
fifty four inch bladed
twelve pound plus
two handed sword
an original Landsknechts
Zweihander Parierhaken
and it took all
his considerable
sword master's skill
and awesome strength
to produce for her
a decent sandwich
especially in slicing
the tomato thinly
perfectly evenly
and removing the
rather hard crust
and neatly
quartering

CLEAR OUT

when he
her ancient
doddering
pensioner husband
actually got it together
to clear out his old junk
books toys rank plimsolls
old medals birds eggs
rotting' Boys Owns'
gasmasks tin helmets
stamp collections
wisdens 1953 etc etc
in great heaps
all his effects of years
she was impressed
but less so
when he ran off
on his 1967
BSA motor bike
with that 1973 blonde
from down the road
without even
saying goodbye

———

SANDS OF TIME

Lately increasingly lately
his sands of time seem
all more frequently
to be including
actually often
all manner
amounts
bits
of
*
:
:
*
of
dust
dross
debris
detritus
sediment
chippings
large lumps
of aggregate
chesils clinker
and non specific
alluvias hardcores
even rocks and slag
and he was becoming
increasingly concerned
about a permanent blockage.

PATRICK ON THE WEB

✳

Film made of the poem *THE DOOR*
recorded by Lawrence Bailey.

Version A
http://vimeo.com/3863672

Version B
http://www.youtube.com/watch?v=HL91uGhY3wo

✳

Reading for the anthology *ON THE DIG*
published by Frisky Moll Press.

http://judithprince.com/section/142974.html

✳

Performance at the Rialto Club, Raynes Park.

http://www.youtube.com/RialtoClub#p/u/1/B8t8fwlEH3w

✳

BIOGRAPHY

Patrick McManus –Survivor poet performer and facilitator- once long ago an architect – lives in Raynes Park with his partner Janet and two cats Asher and VB- Vile Boris – writing performing poetry came as a late surprise – his books 'Delusion of Grandeur' 'Cement and Water' Phantom Rooster Press 'On the Dig' Frisky Moll Press also included in other anthologies to his delight particularly 'Beyond Bedlam' and 'Under The Asylum Tree' and Magma Poetry- also!below

PATRICK MCMANUS— POEMS PUBLISHED IN—   BRIXTON SCHOOL OF BUILDING -1959   LOOSE CHANGE -WAR ON WANT -94   NATIONAL POETRY LIBRARY (USA) -94   DOLE DRUMS -94   GREATER MANCHESTER HUMANIST NEWS -94   SUTTON HUMANIST NEWS -6-94   SUTTON HUMANIST NEWS -10-94   WIMBLEDON GUARDIAN -3-94   LUNATICS LOVERS AND POETS -94   MERTONESQUE -2-95   LONDON 1995 REGIONAL ANTHOLOGY   NATIONAL CONDOM WEEK -BRIT SAFETY CNCIL-8-95   UNDER THE ASYLUM TREE -95   WRITE UP YOUR STREET -MERTON ARTS – 95   POETIC LICENCE -4 -96   SURVIVORS' POETRY 1st NAT JAMBOREE -7-96   SLIPSTREAM -96-97   BEYOND BEDLAM -10-97   PEACE AND FREEDOM -97   POETRY AND PLACE -98   DAIL -DISABILITY ARTS IN LONDON -98   KISSING IN THE DARK -99   SUTTON HUMANIST NEWS -6-99   WWW-METAPHOR /METONYM FOR HEALTH -01 ? PATCHWORK -01   SUTTON HUMANIST -10-01   WWW-SECULARSITES -02   WWW INSTANT ANTHOLOGY cris cheek 11-02   RESOLUTION RIDER-TAXI GALLERY -03-04   WWW-DRUNKEN BOAT -SNAPS -03 SUTTON HUMANISTS AUTUMN -03   MERTON MIND -AG REPORT -03 WWW-HOLEBOOKS-THISISMADNESS dolly sen-03   SHOALHAVEN POEM OF THE WEEK OZ -04   ARA NEWSLETTER -04   WNW -POETS AGAINST THE WAR -04   WWW-SECULARSITES -04   SNAPSHOTS 5-03 > TO DATE RED TOMATOES -04   MAGMA 30 -04-05   WWW PAINSHILL PARK -07-04   WWW-WILD HONEY PRESS SNAPS -05   CEMENT AND WATER -4-06 SUTTON HUMANISTS -10-08   SUTTON HUMANISTS -11-06   SUTTON HUMANISTS -12-06   SUTTON HUMANISTS -1-07   SUTTON HUMANISTS -4-07   SHEFFIELD RADIO -HALO-05-07   WWW-SECULARSITES BRICKS -07   You Tube 'Door McManus' 12-07   MAGA Merton Allotments newsletter-2-08   Poetry Sz -2-08   Poetrykit -2-08   POETRYETC 'POEMS AND POETS' 9-08   WIMBLEDON GUARDIAN 10-08   VIMEO VIDEO -DOOR 4-09   Fiera Lingue -SPRING 4-09   Fiera Lingue-WINTER 4-09   VIMEO L Bailey -DOOR 4-09   MAGA Merton Allotments newsletter-6-09   YOU TUBE RIALTO CLUB -8-09   MAGA Merton Allotments newsletter -10-09 CRUNCHED anthology -10-09   ARA RESIDENTS NEWSLETTER -10-09

Lightning Source UK Ltd.
Milton Keynes UK
25 June 2010

156080UK00001B/4/P

READY MIXED AGGREGATE

＊

＊

＊

POEMS BY PATRICK MCMANUS

Tottie

When She came,
I forgot the pain,
She lay,
And I looked,
Again and again.

A little tot,
Who slept so pure,
But don't
Count on when
She'll get up
To grin anew.

I tried to feed,
And soothe her need,
But she
Wanted more,
And more,
And more!

The little bottle,
Helped her settle,
At night,
With dad,
So I could rest,
Or go out to play.

She filled our lives
Sometimes with cries,
And love,
We will protect,
We'll see her through.

Until
She packs her bags and soars.

Mum's Shortbread

I open the door and am overcome,
Wrapped in warmth.
I am content.
But the aroma of food invites.
My expectation.
Anticipation.
Golden circles of crunchy crispness
Dancing delight.
I reach out…
I feel the light warmth of freshness.
My lips on a sweet powder-ous skin.
Teeth touch the crispy crust.
My mouth fills.
The ecstasy.
The bite.
Crumbs explode within.
Too soon
The delicacy done,
I succumb
       to another one.

Without Whom...

The Marie Curie Nurse arrived,

My angel in disguise,

She quietly took on my role

And I could sleep.

No bed, but blankets, piled up high,

My haven was complete.

At seven I,

Returned to my husband's side.

Another day to savour.

To love.

But all because

I knew

She would come again.

Unfinished Business

Mrs May
Hey
Mrs, Mrs, Mrs May
Go on yersel'.

What?
Mrs May?
A fire Mrs May.
People died Mrs May.
Where were you
Mrs May
Shame on you!

Whatever now Mrs May.
Bloody Hell Mrs May.
Maybe not Mrs May.
Not that way!

Are you listening Mrs May.
How clearly can I say,
Can you hear?
I'm shouting now Mrs May.
I know my mind.
Mrs. Mrs May?

Christ what now Mrs May!
Hey!
Not again Mrs May.
This can't go on,

And on…

And on…

For God's sake Mrs May.
For the country Mrs May.
Think again Mrs May.
Please Mrs May!

No way
Mrs May.
Just…
GO
A
WAY!

Happy New Year

If happy
I knew
You're…
Ready for change.
We shop and cook the old year out,
Then drink the new one in.
Sherry first to start the night
With poise and grand-eur,
Then on to wine, a white or red,
Full bodied dilutes sauterne.
The spirit then can gently flow
With juice or coke or lime.
The evening is awash with
Friends who grasp and dash
"You mind the time?"
The party travels on,
The drinks are less refined,
A swig of whisky, vodka or rum,
Grasped in greeting,
Or fortify a farewell,
The welcome undoes your heart,
Forever heading home.
But when morning comes all hazy grey,
I wonder -
"What day is it today?"

Leveling

The judge sits up high
On a bench.
Overseeing his court for the day.
We try not to catch his eye.
He shifts in his seat.
A cough covered embarrassment,
He's farted again.

As the smell drifts down to those at the front,
Eyes twinkle,
Hankies rise,
He announces,
With precision and grace.
"It wasn'y me."

He Came to Tea

My arm at the ready.
He was quite unaware.
Blinkered to my world.
"Is the tea made?"

I don't get the tea
Said the daughter to me
I know what you mean I replied.

The ritual requires hot water
In the pot by itself.
Then the kettle re-boils.
Tea goes inside with the water
Just boiled.
It sits for a while.

You see, making tea is an art.
Taking time,
Infusing
Then oozing like gold.
Into a fine bone china cup.

Whenever,
He came to tea.

Unknown device!

Tower over the keyboard,
Monitor the mouse.
Purge all.

Monitor the tower,
Mouse beside the keyboard.
Save yourself.

Monitor all keyboards,
Towering mouse found.
Warning.

Click here to begin.

B. Patient

I want to go outside.
The window lets me see,
Raindrop dappled pavement
Reflecting sombre skies.
Can I go outside?

I want to smell the air.
Feel the cool and rinsing rain.
Taste a drop of nature.
Touch nothingness again.
Can I go out there?

Healthy bodies have freedoms.
That luck you never know,
Until it's taken.
Then you learn,
How to stay inside.

Visitors Call

Visitors call and bravely chat,
What can you do and when do you nap,
Where is your pain and is it too bad,
When the visitors call and bravely chat.

The doctor will call and quietly check,
Where is your pain and what do you eat,
Double the dose any day if you need,
When the doctor will call and quietly check.

The nurse will call and happily chat,
The family are all included in that,
She checks medication and changes the pads,
When the nurse does call everyone can laugh.

The parent does call (but not much of that)
It is stiff upper lip and tea and light chat,
I do hope the medicine will soon take effect,
When the parent does call we pretend all that.

The brother will call at least once in the year,
The bedroom is visited and the emotion is real,
The questions are asked and the answers are clear,
The tears of the brother show you are dear.

The wife will be by your side all the time,
Gentle and caring and keeping you fine,
Sharing those moments so precious and dear,
The wife won't go anywhere "don't you fear."

The daughter will be in and sit by your side,
Not understanding but not wanting to hide,
Watching your movements and needing you near,
The daughter is bravely learning and facing her
fear.

Resting

The sun got me up
For a walk with the dog,
Before cooking and shopping
For lunch,
As you, at your home, lay in bed.

Shovel coal on the fire,
Fill the kettle,
Put on a bright smile,
Say hello
To you, as you lay in your bed.

I'd tidy the papers,
Reorder the fridge,
Check your medication,
As you continue to lie in your bed.

Just ready to go,
The first breath of goodbye,
And the crossword is proffered.
And you continued to lie in your bed.

I'd start with the blanks,
Then shake my head,
Then suggest that some might be wrong.
You would smile and agree from your bed.

It might take an hour
To disentangling myself,
Leaving everything set
So that you could comfortably rest in your
bed.

And then there was scrabble…
Forty minutes an average
For thirty rounds
Those were played from your bed.

Looking back it seems mad.
You watched,
And we danced to your tune.
And you lay, at your home, in your bed.

Eczema

Prickling on my torso,
A telling tickle,
Itches just below a strap.

Remove the strap,
Just scratch.
Scratchy, scratchy, scratch.

The micro-organisms cause a rampaging
riot,
Blotches billow angry,
Gnawing on my brain,
Which says:
Do not scratch!
No – don't, don't scratch.
I said…
No scratching!
Scratchy, scratch, scratch

Will you never learn?
The skin is thin.
Bloodied skin.

A recycled
Torture.

The doctors

First was the doctor you can see every day
He sent you away.
Second was the doctor who looked at your
blood
He wanted to know more.
Third was the doctor in on the scan,
HE TOOK YOU ASIDE AND HELD YOUR
HAND.
Fourth was the specialist distant and grand,
She told you a story that melted your guts.

Then it was nurses injecting the stuff,
A determined legion fighting and rough,
Your hair all fell out and you looked pretty
grim,
But we prayed it was working, took it on the
chin.

Things got better we planned for some fun
But before that happened you
went
back
to the doctor you can see every day.

Internal bleeding was our next diagnosis,
Curing this had to be a serious business.

Next was the doctor you met on the ward,
He was quiet and listened as your story was
told.
He smiled and offered ideas of reprieve,
You listened and hoped he was to be believed.
Next was the doctor you met for some therapy.
You rushed in for 3 minutes and went on your
way,
Returning weekly with not much to say.

The bleeding has stopped they happily said.
We returned to our home breathing again.
The story continues with not much to report,
The decline was slow and we didn't go back
To the doctors in town.

We stuck with our doctor that we could see
everyday
There was only a problem when he was away.
A stranger would come and think we wanted
lies and they
Told us stories we knew were awry.

One day you developed a serious pain,
They took you by ambulance that day.

I stayed at home.

When I phoned to find out what was amiss
A very young doctor said this.
As your life dwindled away,
"The prognosis is not good."

Well, what could I say?

Force Eight Imminent: Rockall, Malin, Hebrides...

Clouds roll thick insulating and grey,
Menacing the sun-bleached vista.
Pixels of rain angled curtains snaking my way.
They bully off-course a push or a pull,
A spear with a fierce frenzied force.

The haul to the beach keeps me,
buckled and bent,
sandblasted and breathless,
hair matted – unkempt.
Sandstorms skitter,
Smart in attack.
Leaving tear tingled eyelines,
from wind-blown flak.

Avoiding the spume,
And the wet sinky sand.
Fly like a yacht running free,
Up the deep powdered strand.
Drowning in drifts,
Sand dunes resigned
Softly smoothed over
Yesterday's redefined.

Tormented inland,
Past the grey stooping grass,
Prickled and prodded – as you pass.
Then,
Tacking leeward,
And home.

Halting

Do not come to see me die,

It would be to tell another ugly lie,

Attempt disguise to the hurt you served on me,

I felt it all.

And yet I kept your secret gnawing hidden,

Locked in my perplexed heart

Resilience, love and truth absorbed it all.

Do not come close.

Do not come to see me die.

Friends?

Come in.
Sit before my blazing fire.
Eat from my table,
Rest your weary head.
Be nurtured.
Again…
Again..
Again.
Let my love oil your cracking twisted soul.

But
When I needed something back…
I never heard you call.
I never felt your hand,
Nor smelt your breath.
Instead you veiled a dagger,
To prick.
To pierce.
To hurt.
Again…
Again.

But never reach to ease my aches
Nor dry my tears.

Vicious vibe mocked feeble footsteps.
You trampled.
You spat.
You scythe my strength.
And undermine.
Again…

Apples

When he died he left some love with me.
But You tried to rip it all away.
You told the world, you took control,
You covered up the truth.
You never soothed.
You never held my hand.
You never wept with me.

You licked his stamps, pinned on his broach,
Cashed his cheque for sixteen grand.
Then scuttled back to hide your head
Beneath your desk.
And when I asked a question you...
You turned your back and caterwauled my name.
You never spoke.
You never touched my face.
You never wept with me.

You told such lies.
Did you know they would make me cry?
How could you say that I agreed?
You never spoke.
You never asked.
You never eased my pain.

Life teaches us about the myths.
You failed the scales of the just,
To uphold the law.
You, and you...
But remember this,
We never heard.
Because,
We never spoke.
That's why,
We never agreed

The Bay

Wind combs my hair backwards,

My face sandblasted red,

My eyes smart and,

Weeping,

Bullied by the wind,

Bowing,

Coorie doon,

In the sand dunes

Where green grass blows grey.

Noticing

We never said,

But we knew.

Expensive champagne!

For us two.

Stored in the rack.

Birds are for chasing

Birds are for chasing,
I'm sure you know.
They sit on the beach,
Just waiting for you to show.
Waiting and watching and dipping their toes,
Certain, no worries, anticipation will grow.

You slobber expectant,
Watchful and aware,
My wellies are standing
Right outside the door.
My jacket is lifted,
You sit and attend.
Walkies are cited you comprehend.

You hit the beach running,
As fast as you can.
The birds sit pretending
Its catch if you can.
They tempt you to thunder
All the way to the shore,
Before they rise laughing,
They've got you, like before.

They skim and they glide,
Over water and sand,
You are always just behind them,
But they have the upper hand.
The gulls play to frustrate you,
Pairing their game,
One sitting and resting

The other takes aim.
They cackle and call to the world
All around,

To see this mad fool,
That thinks little, just dashes round,
And around,
And around.

You tire of your running,
The birds all know
You're beaten and cowed,
They temp you to get them,
Just one last go.

I call you to come
And set off to the car.
Another walk over,
Your attend to my call.
We'll be back here tomorrow,
No vary to that,
A dog lives in the moment,
No secret, a fact.

'Football and girls is fine until...'

Her long hair swung on the follow through and she scored.

The kitchen…
Get back inside,
Make some scones.
The aroma of nurture
Is right for a girl.

The boots!
Football boots
Made for men.
Men with speed
Kicking balls

The Game
Beautiful
Each city will echo
See scarves in the air
Hear the roar.

Did I hear you right?
Did you say?
'It's not the right
place
for a girl.

You say
I can choose…
Either your wife,
Or I play.

Curling

The air is chilled,
Eight players group.
The coin is tossed,
Stones slide,
And glide,
Tap, rest
Or take away.
The tactics test
Your skill.
Delivery slow,
With little weight
You draw in to win.
Your stone survives,
Is guarded,
All others swept by.

Next end again.
Skip calls,
Roaring and loud
But.
The ice doesn't play,
As the stone hangs out.
Again,
You take aim.
Sweepers sweeping away,
You touch red and roll,
Behind a guard,
Taking the final end.
A hand shake
Acknowledges.
Your glory is hailed.
Good Game.
Good Game.

The Dean Gallery

Grand, finished, stone blocked and formal,
A staircase of precision and invitation,
The entrance is empty,
Instructions on show.
No guidance is given - they expect you to know.
The teenage invigilator peeps out from Room One,
No smile.
No order given.
Just a job being done.
I want to start laughing – a urinal,
I can't believe what I see,
So numerous the framings,
All just superb and so grand,
The value phenomenal.
What cost for just one?

I see Dali and Miro and Cher…
Max Ernst, Man Rae and Picasso,
Giacometti and Jackson Pollock,
Others I know but now have forgotten,
So much to see and a lifetime to know.

The work is sensational in 2010,
Challenging and original,
So, what was the greeting back when
The work was freshly on show.

I am shocked by the dolls,
Angered and challenged,
What response would yield
From my gran?
Another World?
Thank-you.

Mein Gott

Here.
Mile on mile where,
Rumbling motors skirt the bay,
Dodging unfettered sheep,
Who wander,
Roasted beneath an unmasked sun,
Over the low tide sweep of,
Copious casings of crustaceans,
Amid,
Parched porcelain chips,
And clouded sea glass.
On grains of fine crushed coral.
Grains deep on grains,
Patterned,
Undulations,
Set by the distant tide.
Baked brittle.
A pie-crust:
With a pearly glaze,
That glistens in moonlight.
Ever grinding,
Regenerating,
Forever Gott Bay.

Exploited Innocence

Imponderable

Enigmatic

Absurdity

Immeasurable impenetrable naivety

Raw inexperience meets proficiency

Unthinking

Impulsive survival endured

Imponderable values meet inconsequential youth

Immeasurable endurance of life.

Impenetrable naivety meets the face of survival.

Impenetrable naivety meets men.

Immeasurable innocence exploited

The Birthday

We get our festive day
The cards come bowling in
Anyone who misses the date
Knows to
Apologise…
And not forget again.
As years go by,
The dates engrain.
The trigger never fails.
Until.
The ones you love pass on.
Their age no longer hailed,
And yet,
The date stands proud,
Shouts out,,
But

You whisper out their name.

Dead Space

I wake and in the morning gloom or light I see the space
you left. You left your space to me and yet I know it's
yours. I filled my wardrobe full and now my clothes all
hang, more room than they need. Your space is in here too.
I organise my shoes they stand together waiting for their
time to come, to take me out. Your shoes could wait here
too. I do not need more shoes. I only have two feet and
they can only wear two shoes. The rest are just for show.
They could all go into your box.

I organise my makeup. It stands and prettily balances up a
space that always was mine. How often does that space
create the face you knew? My days to dance and play are
gone with you. You know you can come back and have
this space. I will not mind. Your pillow waits each night
for a head to cushion, a cheek to flatten or your hair to
crush.

Your space is still. Your space is saved. Your space is here.

I saw the farmer standing...

The grey of his eyes in step with his worn-out speech.
And it was May.
His sober tale told of cracks – so deep – so wide and the
roots so dry.
And the forecaster's pessimism thundering down.
No end they said, examples – impossible – dripped on.
No-one shall waste a drop.
No hosepipes!
Debate ensued from every garden gate as water trickled
from watering cans.
And it was June.
Rain came – North to South and East to West – a heavy
shaft of gloom.
And the grey clouds burst and burst again, washing wet
the land.
The dry fields sucked in the first and then it fell, again and
again and again.
Dampness turned to dripping then to drenched.
Awash became a pool and then a flood, a swollen lake.
July and August sheltered beneath an umbrella.
And then,
I saw the farmer standing, the red of his eyes met the
catch in his voice.
And he was done!

My Garden

A glow of pleasure,
Felt inside,
When I think of Eccles Mains.
The garden grew from the tractors plough,
To the ordered flowered reins,
Of human toil.
The winter was the placid time,
When the weather worked for free,
The weeds curtailed their healthy game,
Giving me a few months of reprieve.
The trees and shrubs refined their style.
With a windy brushing down,
With snow and ice to trim their guile,
Forcing some down to the ground.
I await the spring with excited fear,
I'll survey my damaged dream.
And start again this arduous task,
The unfettered gardeners goal.

The I-Café

The café's clean and quiet hub sucked me in.
The clientele sat silent before their silent screen.
A private view.
How nice,
I thought to watch a film.
The cappuccino's creamy foam was just the thing.
But my screen refused to play!
Even with a stealthy stab.
How embarrassing,
When I hoped to copy others.
My shifty presence – unnoticed.
Close attention – then try again.
I put my glasses on.
How simple,
I thought, to switch it on.
A message with instructions seemed so clear.
And yet my comprehension failed
…a number?

Not been before ma dear? See your receipt.
I smile, I nod and understand.
Finding the number to type.
How cool.
I thought
I now was one of them.

Bad Weather

Where were you when the snow began?
I called you up and your phone rang.
I nursed the fire and watched it fall,
A beautiful blanket covering all.

I judged the sky: soft steely grey,
It stayed just like that all day.
When I went to bed my mind was numb,
Snow fresh and deep would curtail my fun.

The roads are full of the fluffy stuff.
My car loses grip not straightening up,
To get out of the drive,
I get out my shovel and dig.

Safe

The lighthouse stands,

He volunteers his guard.

Day, night, dusk or dawn,

His eye is on.

His constant pulse,

Smells danger in the wind,

Clockwork timing,

Sooths the path,

In sea-soaked days.

The lighthouse stands,

Nature unchecked.

A phenomenon

Of man.

Sunset on Balephetris

The black rock's height of overbearing past lets me
rest, my presence light, to watch the sun reflect.
The here and now, visual savouring of golden reds slip
low, a crimson wash completes the glow.
The ageless landscape dipped in heat, oblivious to my
short repose and my footsteps instant dry.

I left the camera sitting in the hall – at home.

The camera I failed to bring,
Will always have an absent file,
Unnamed - June 2011.
As the ferry crossed the regatta-ed minch,
Dolphins arch and leap and dive,
And total fifty-four.
So early morning snaps of nature,
On the run.
Were missed.

The rain set in and indoor work began.
But by the evening - warm sunshine and,
I missed a photo of a bird.
A heron stood like stone as my shadow slipped on by.
The shock was when I watched a tern dive down.
The heron stood and took this wild attack,
Silent, strong and still.
The tern set down on sand nearby,
to watch this heron,
Who had defied his will.

A hollow echoed bellow from a,
Seal across the bay drew me on.
I walked the tide washed sand.
The seals bellied over isles of rock.
Dipping down to swim.
Came up so near -
A head on show to pose.
And see no camera!

Washed up beyond the high tide mark,
A carcass rots.
At five foot long.
I spied the jaw so full of needled teeth,
No camera to record this nature's saw.
The rotted flesh will be cast afar when I return,
With my camera.

That night as gloomy midnight set.
The sky stayed light and clear.
A hare sat,
On the grassy knoll right outside my door.
His ears lay calm.
No snap to capture his athletic core.
The corncrake teases with his scratching call.
I wait.
A sighting's bound to be tonight.
When my camera's not there.

Day by Day…

The steel grey sea strokes the ice white sky and the air
bites and nips.

The iron studden sky hangs with tragedy, and the sea lies
silent in fear.

The rolling melancholy of the sky is so close that the sea
spits and foams, enraged.

Today
The sky dawns pastel blue over an undulating mirror of
purity.

to be continued…

Coronovirus 19 Perhaps?

Sense is good.
Think and beware.
Take advice.
And hear
The lessons of others.

That holiday you wanted
Will cost you dear.
That car you tested
Will be cheaper next year.
Remember
Something unexpected
May happen
          tomorrow....

The Show-Off

The red light instructs
We stop on the line.
Engines whine.
Feathering toes.
Breaking time.
Eying round.
Gear box slips.
Set to go.

First away.
Jump ahead.
Cool.

Dudes on show.

Family

In the office they laugh.
And the story she tells passes on.
Ridiculed relations.
'Not a patch on you…'
Your pristine halo shines through.

But I ask to the night…
Where were you when he cried
When he asked for our help.
When his ways waivered.

So, I advised.
Spend your money.
Take independence back.
I'll take the flack when you're done.

Just a Jealous Guy

'...just like you always do...'
'...no-one likes you...'
'...you poison the air that I breathe...'

Do I understand.
I am that one.

Everyone a threat.
In me... you see you.
You want me to be you.

Your defamation
A disguise
Of envy.
Your life is a search for...
Whatever you never had.

And I understand.

Waiting

Thrummm, Thrummm,
Tap...Tap...Tap,
Thrum
The clock hovers over quarter past.
Feel a hot flush creep.
I supress the scream.
As a booth stands empty.
Thrumm, Thrumm,
Tap...Tap...Tap...

Breathe in
Breathe out.
1...2...3...

Memories

A chord of music chaunts...

A touch transcends...

A scent stirs...

An apparition

Prompts the
Buried images, always present,
To writhe again.
Breathe.
Like a soldier,
Primed.
From my watchtower on the past.

Christmas

Remember the year of Richard's new bike.
And the memorial we gave
To the little old dear
And her imagined fate.

The Christmas jigsaws that grew and grew.
Betty got tiddly
On Keith's home-made brew
Or Campari.

Teenager's in fashion from Biba,
Would glide down the stairs:
Golden chords,
Painted eyes,
Ziggy Star-dusted air.

The year of the balloon
Brian crafted his beast
On the breakfast room table.
But it's launch was at night.
When it flew to the stars.

Helen's musical refrain,
Two Little Boys,
Shang-a-lang,
Hey Jude,
Again.
On a loop from the front room.

And with Mag,
Christmas Eve angels
Out in the snow
At midnight.

Always,
A walk in the woods.
Find a tree on its side
And we'd fight – King or Queen.

Boogie-Woogie filled space,
Before games.
The Family Coach to the Shops…
Or the stations.
But the best was the last.
Balloon Ball!

All that excitement
Flourished
In your front room at Christmas.

Wounded

They announce it all and it hurts.
354 schoolboys' eyes
Share the joke.
Graffiti a name in a book
An unashamed sharing.
But no-one calls them out.

I know.
It happened back then.

At home relaxed and funny
We watch them learn to cope
With the outside world.
At school the jungle's untamed.
Uninhibited.
Uncontrolled.
Unseen.
Chafing teenage angst:
For the fat ones, the thin ones,
The outspoken grotesque ones,
The 'in' ones, the spare ones,
The anorexic 'in care' ones,
And the disabled enabled to share.
See them laugh!

We all know.
We carry the scars.

Being There

You peer out from your being.
Lost in the layers of life.
Lost to yourself.
'You remember….'
He asks.
See a smile of surprize
And wonder
Listening enrapt
Engaged
He has a story to repeat
Visitors hear it
Again
And again
Until it too is lost
In the layers of life.
So, we begin again
'You remember…'

To Rob

My love of 34 years
richly smoulders anew.
From tentative kisses in a stairwell
you gently climbed into my heart.

You orchestrated the soundtrack to our life,
Of varied vista,
Of hard graft,
Musically merged with silvery sands
And a sparkling spangled sea
Carpeted our world.
The best
Wildly wet, windy and wearied.

We have had so much my love.

I would have more.

My life, my love, is you.

Russet   X

Printed in Great Britain
by Amazon